M000202876

POCKET IRIS WISDOM

WITTY QUOTES AND WISE WORDS FROM IRIS APFEL

POCKET IRIS WISDOM

WITTY QUOTES AND WISE WORDS FROM IRIS APFEL

hardie grant books

CONTENTS

IRIS APFEL ON...

Y LE

“ ”

The worst fashion faux pas is looking in the mirror and seeing somebody else.

Dazed & Confused, November 2012

"

If you want personal style, you can't copy anyone else or it's not personal style anymore.

....
Yahoo!, 25th May 2015

" "

I think style implies originality and thoughtfulness and an expression of one's self, not just being a fashion plate – which is a very nice thing to be, but that's not style.

Stylecaster, February 2016

Style is attitude, attitude, attitude.

Red, 28th July 2015

" "

There are a lot of people out there who put a lot of effort into looking awful.

Dazed & Confused, November 2012

" "

Taste you can learn. But style is like charisma. You know it when you see it.

....
Architectural Digest, 31st May 2011

"　**"**

If you're not comfortable in your own skin, you won't be comfortable in your own clothes.

....

Racked, 9th September 2014

" "

If you don't expand your waistline, you can expand your closet, which is better.

The Martha Stewart Show, 2011

" "

I love a timeless look...
I can mix something
I bought last week
with something I've
hoarded for 30 years.

Panache, September 2005

" "

I like to mix up everything. And then hopefully my love binds it all together and it comes out right.

....

Interview at the Tate Modern, 23rd April 2014

" "

If someone says, 'Buy this, you'll be stylish,' you won't be stylish because you won't be you. You have to learn who you are first and that's painful.

Telegraph, 23rd October 2011

"

Fashion can be bought, but style is in your genes.

....

French Elle, 19th February 2016

" "

The way you dress shows who you are and who you want to be.

Elle, December 2011

" "

The fashion police are not going to come and take you away. And if they do, you might have some fun in jail.

Interview at the Metropolitan Museum of Art, 17th June 2012

" "

My mother worshipped at the altar of the accessory.

....

Women's Hour, 31st July 2015

I'm a hopeless romantic. I buy things because I fall in love with them.

Guardian, 13th March 2012

" "

The fun of getting dressed is it's a creative experience.

Interview at the Peabody Essex Museum,
23rd October 2009

" "

I'm not pretty, and I'll never be pretty, but it doesn't matter. I have something much better. I have style.

....

Iris, directed by Albert Maysles, 2014

IRIS APFEL ON...

UALITY

" "

If you're going to sit there and do the same damn thing all the time, you might as well jump into the box yourself.

....

Iris, directed by Albert Maysles, 2014

I don't like the norm.

The Coveteur, 7th April 2014

" "

I think it's an awful thing to look like everybody else.

Sportswear International, 8th July 2015

" "

**People have called
me an artist and said I
use myself as a canvas.
I never considered
myself... I guess I am
an artist because I do
a lot of artistic things.**

Hunger, 29th December 2015

" "

I always tell people to follow their dreams, to be true to themselves, and not just be carbon copies of what they think they should be, because then they'll go through life miserable.

AnOther, 29th July 2015

"

When you don't dress like everybody else, you don't have to think like everybody else.

The New York Times, 25th August 2011

" "

Doing your own thing is very good, if you have a thing to do.

....

Observer, 17th January 2010

" "

I like individuality. It's so lost these days. There's so much sameness, everything is homogenised.

....

Iris, directed by Albert Maysles, 2014

IRIS APFEL ON...

VE

"

Love is wonderful. I think it's mutuality, liking the same things, having respect for each other.

....

Interview with Duro Olowu, 6th June 2013

" "

[My husband Carl] was sharp as a tack, and he always looked like a dude.

....

T Magazine, 26th August 2015

❝ ❞

[On her husband Carl]

I figured he was cool, and he was cuddly, and he cooked Chinese, so I couldn't do any better.

Iris, directed by Albert Maysles, 2014

" "

Sex has something to do with it, but real love is not sex.

Interview with Duro Olowu, 6th June 2013

" "

I was asked today by some pretty young lady if I'd give them some dating advice ... I told them to put down their cell phones.

The Telegraph, 28th March 2016

"

I always say my husband has given me all the space I need, except in the closet.

Yahoo!, 25th May 2015

" "

It's much easier to jump into somebody's pants than to get into somebody's head.

....
Interview with Duro Olowu, 6th June 2013

The secret to lasting love is being kind to each other.

Red, 28th July 2015

IRIS APFEL ON...

WING DER

" "

**Just because you get to
a certain number doesn't
mean you have to roll
up into a ball and wait
for the grim reaper.**

Dazed & Confused, November 2012

I'm the world's oldest living teenager.

Newsweek, 23rd August 2013

Getting older ain't for sissies, I'll tell you.

Into the Gloss, January 2012

" "

The fashion industry doesn't just forget old people, it forgets middle-aged people. The fashion industry is youth obsessed, which is totally insane from a financial point of view so I don't feel sorry for them, they brought it on themselves.

The Telegraph, 28th March 2016

"

In the words of my grandpa: 'a woman is as old as she looks, but a man is never old until he stops looking.'

Iris, directed by Albert Maysles, 2014

" "

I think as you get older,
you should use less and
less make-up. Unless
you know how to apply
it very artfully, you could
end up looking like an
old turtle.

Lucky Shops, 5th December 2012

"   "

If you hang around long enough, everything comes back.

....

Iris, directed by Albert Maysles, 2014

" "

I'm a great believer in common sense, and the older I get, I see that common sense is not that common.

AnOther, 29th July 2015

" "

At my stage of the game, if I don't have fun, I don't want to do it.

Sportswear International, 8th July 2015

Retirement is a fate worse than death.

Daily Life, 7th February 2016

" "

It's ridiculous, this idea that once you reach a certain age you are ready for the junk, that being old is somehow dirty and disgusting. The alternative to old is not very pleasant.

Iris, directed by Albert Maysles, 2014

"

If God is good enough to give you those years, flaunt them.

....

The Times, 30th July 2015

SELF

"

I'm experimental, I'm curious, and I try things. And if I like it, I do it again!

The Talks, 15th February 2016

" "

People would always say to me, 'Why are you wearing such large frames?' And I would say, 'The bigger to see you.'

Interview Magazine, 29th April 2015

"   "

If people don't like it, it's their problem, not mine.

Interview with Duro Olowu, 6th June 2013

I'm not a minimalist, as I'm sure you've noticed.

The Coveteur, 7th April 2014

"

I love being busy, I think it keeps me alive. I'm probably the busiest person you ever heard of.

....

People, 19th February 2016

" "

I've been collecting accessories since I was 11 years old, creeping around flea markets and sales and everything. Whenever I saw unusual eyeglass frames, I bought them. Occasionally, I would wear them just as an accessory without any lenses.

Interview, 29th April 2015

" "

I don't play cards, I don't play golf, I don't like to go to ladies' luncheons – to me, that's a fate worse than death – and this gives me purpose.

Newsweek, 23rd August 2013

" "

[My look is] either very baroque or very zen – everything in between makes me itch.

The New York Times, 17th November 2005

" "

I don't describe my style – I don't think it's my place. That's for other people to do.

....

W Magazine, 21st March 2016

"

I don't have any rules because I would only be breaking them.

···

Iris, directed by Albert Maysles, 2014

" "

Technologically, I live in the 17th century.

....

Marie Claire, 2nd October 2015

Caviar is my drug of choice.

In conversation with Ari Seth Cohen,
28th September 2012

" "

I was probably the first woman to wear jeans.

Iris, directed by Albert Maysles, 2014

" "

I haven't had an average day in my life.

....
Yahoo!, 25th May 2015

“ ,,

Sometimes I feel stretched to pieces: my head is in the clouds, but my feet are on the ground.

....
Jezebel, 27th April 2015

" "

I don't expect to find inspiration. It just sort of comes. Sometimes you step on a bug and you get inspired.

Newsweek, 23rd August 2013

66 99

They're carrying on about me as if I invented penicillin.

....

Vanity Fair, 29th April 2015

I'm Iris Apfel, geriatric starlet.

Condé Naste Traveller, 10th June 2015

FE

"

Getting dressed up to go to a party is often more fun than going to the party.

Blackbook, 29th April 2015

" "

If your hair is done properly and you're wearing good shoes, you can get away with anything.

....

Footwear News, 6th February 2012

" "

You really don't own anything... you're only here for a short time, so you kind of rent it.

....

Interview with Duro Olowu, 6th June 2013

It's better to be happy than well-dressed.

Iris, directed by Albert Maysles, 2014

Colour can raise
the dead.

···

Iris, directed by Albert Maysles, 2014

" "

To lead the good life in New York, the two most important things for a woman are a chauffeur and a fur-lined raincoat. If you have those two things, you're made.

....
Newsweek, 23rd August 2013

"   "

If you can't be pretty, you have to make yourself attractive.

Observer, 17th January 2010

Keep your ears and eyes open. And don't lose your passion.

Red, 28th July 2015

" "

Everything that's important in my life has happened by accident.

....

T Magazine, 9th January 2014

You can't be interesting if you're not interested.

Red, 28th July 2015

" **"**

Fantasy is powerful, powerful, powerful. And everybody can't handle it in big doses, but you can try little bits at a time.

....

In conversation with Tavi Gevinson,
reported by *Racked*, 18th June 2012

“ ”

Life is grey and dull; you might as well have a little fun when you dress.

Iris, directed by Albert Maysles, 2014

" "

More is more and less is a bore.

··

Advanced Style, 2nd October 2012